IMAGES
of America

CATHOLIC UTAH

T0287182

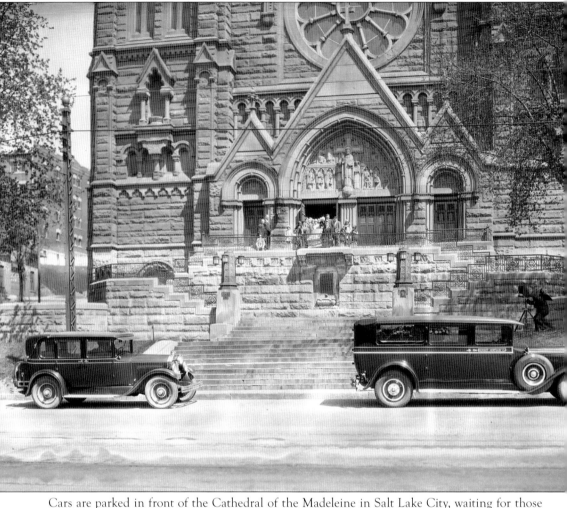

Cars are parked in front of the Cathedral of the Madeleine in Salt Lake City, waiting for those attending the 1929 funeral of John Bilboa. (Utah State Historical Society.)

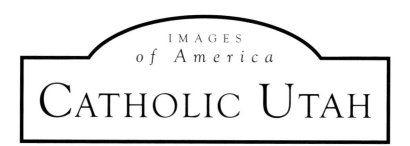

IMAGES
of America

CATHOLIC UTAH

Colleen McDannell

ARCADIA
PUBLISHING

Copyright © 2023 by Colleen McDannell
ISBN 978-1-4671-6062-9

Published by Arcadia Publishing
Charleston, South Carolina

Printed in the United States of America

Library of Congress Control Number: 2023939296

For all general information, please contact Arcadia Publishing:
Telephone 843-853-2070
Fax 843-853-0044
E-mail sales@arcadiapublishing.com

Visit us on the Internet at www.arcadiapublishing.com

*To my friend Robert A. Orsi, who transformed
the study of American Catholicism*

CONTENTS

Acknowledgments

There are so many people I need to thank for making this book possible. Michael L. Cortney, director of archives and records for the Diocese of Salt Lake City not only patiently found images for me but scanned them. Sarah Langsdon, head of special collections at Weber State University, and Reese Julian, assistant director of Giovale Library at Westminster College, promptly responded to my emails to reproduce photographs. At the Uintah County Regional History Center, Michelle Fuller rescanned images so they could be published. In Indiana, Cindy Hamill, director of the congregational archives and records of Sisters of the Holy Cross made her rich collection available to me. Several archivists at St. Benedict's Monastery in St. Joseph, Minnesota, searched for photographs for me and answered questions. Jeff Hoffman, director of archives for Our Lady of Victory Missionary Sisters, helped me identify sisters in photographs and sent me valuable information about their missions in Utah. Sister Mary Harper sent me materials regarding the Franciscan Sisters of Atonement. I am especially appreciative of Forest Cuch and Larry Cesspooch, who clarified native American Catholic life in eastern Utah. Finally, my colleagues in the Department of History were generous with their time. Paul Reeve read through the final manuscript with his characteristic care and thoroughness, and Greg Smoak helped me understand the Indigenous people of Utah. Thanks to all.

The images in this volume appear courtesy of the Congregation of the Sisters of the Holy Cross, Notre Dame, Indiana (SHC); Diocese of Salt Lake City, Office of Archives and Records (DSLC); Sisters of the Order of Saint Benedict, St. Joseph, Minnesota (SSB); Special Collections, J. Willard Marriott Library, the University of Utah (UU); Uintah County Library Regional History Center (UCL); Utah State Historical Society (USHS), Special Collections Department, Stewart Library, Weber State University (WSU); and Westminster College, Giovale Library (WC).

INTRODUCTION

Catholic Utah begins with the heart of Catholicism, the experience of the divine. As early as 1776, the Mexican Franciscans Atanasio Domínguez and Silvestre Vélez de Escalante not only explored the territory of what would become Utah, but they began each day with prayers, the rosary, and litanies. As they moved westward from Santa Fe, New Mexico, they named every mountain, lake, river, and arroyo after the Virgin Mary and their favorite saints. Through naming, they linked the unfamiliar space to a society of the holy, thus making the landscape sacred and meaningful to the newcomers. But, unlike in other parts of the West, the Franciscans did not build missions. It would take another hundred years before Catholics would permanently settle on land settled by Native peoples and claimed by the Mormons. From the first church dedicated in 1871, through the wooden churches lovingly built by miners, to the stately Cathedral of the Madeleine, Catholics sought to worship God in sacred spaces set apart from the everyday. And yet, their rituals and worship drew out of their churches. By the 1930s, Paulist priests would preach from trailers hauled behind their cars. In the 1940s, Trappist monks would chase the monastery's stray cattle on horseback. *Catholic Utah* ends in 1976 when over 13,000 Catholics traveled across the state to participate in a bicentennial celebratory Mass staged event in the Salt Palace convention hall. Although still a minority religion in Utah, Catholics had proudly established their ways of worshiping God in spaces throughout the state.

Loving God with one's heart, soul, and mind is the first of the two great commandments. The second great commandment is to love one's neighbor. From displaying the love of God, *Catholic Utah* moves to showing how the community demonstrated the love of neighbor. In 1873, when Fr. (later bishop) Lawrence Scanlan arrived in Salt Lake City, he had two goals: to free the existing church from debt and to establish a school. He arranged for Sisters of the Holy Cross from far away Indiana to open a private academy for girls. Education was to engage the spirit, the mind, and the body and was meant not only for Catholics. From Father Scanlan and the sisters' perspective, it was simply an act of charity to offer the possibility of conversion to Utah's Latter-day Saints and Protestants. Catholic education in Utah reveals the intense commitment of women religious. For instance, the Franciscan Sisters of Atonement taught summer school in rural Utah towns to prepare children to receive the sacraments, and the Daughters of Charity staffed a parish school in Price. In 1927, the Sisters of Perpetual Adoration came from Mexico to teach vocational skills to the growing Spanish-speaking community. Until the number of sisters declined in the 1970s, Catholic education in Utah was the domain of women.

Catholic healing was also under the control of women religious. Since Jesus healed the sick, so should his followers. Shortly after Holy Cross Sisters established St. Mary's Academy, others from the order founded a hospital. By the late 19th century, mining had become an important Utah industry, and many of the miners were Irish and Italian Catholics. However, what had originally been an effort to attend to their needs evolved into a fashionable and effective hospital offering care for all. Holy Cross Sisters (and after World War II Benedictines in Ogden) not only staffed hospitals as nurses, they were also cagey administrators who hired and fired male doctors. Many of Utah's nurses were educated in their schools. Sisters filled their hospitals with Catholic iconography. They established values of cleanliness, orderliness, and efficiency while seeking to balance modern science with compassionate and humane care. To support their hospitals, Catholic laymen and laywomen gave of their time and treasure. As with education, however, the declining number of sisters accompanied the rising cost of medical care. Hospitals once run by Catholics were sold.

A similar process occurred as women religious cared for orphans, the elderly, the disabled, and those Catholics outside of the parish structure. For instance, St. Ann's orphanage was established in 1891 by Holy Cross Sisters, with their 1900 building funded by mining magnate Thomas Kearns. The orphanage not only cared for children who had no parents but also for those whose parents were too poor to care for them. However, by the 1950s, national standards of child welfare had changed. Federal and state funding for dependent children as well as foster care was replacing orphanages. In addition, the diocese was trying to coordinate its caring under a priest-directed "Catholic Charities." In 1954, Kearns-St. Ann's Orphanage closed, and the building turned into a parochial school. Caring continued but focused on new needs: Native American teens in an Indian boarding school, prisoners, and refugees.

To coordinate and inspire the love of God and of neighbor required the committed leadership of many men and women. Leading an ethnically diverse community made up of people from many different social classes was no easy task. Bishops had to fund and manage parishes located far from each other. They had to find Catholic religious orders to run needed schools, hospitals, and charitable institutions. Most critically, they had to provide certain sacraments and see to the spiritual lives of their flock. There never were enough priests to minister to the sparsely distributed community of Catholics, although the number of clergymen grew from 35 in 1939 to 81 in 1957. Laymen and laywomen, consequently, had to take on leadership roles in their parishes. Their responsibilities would increase after the Second Vatican Council encouraged all to participate in the mystical Body of Christ.

Catholic Utah concludes with an underacknowledged element of religious life: enjoyment and entertainment. Parishes and schools were places of spiritual and intellectual uplift, but they also were places for simply having fun. Catholics worked hard at fundraising for their institutions not only because it was the right thing to do but because it brought them together with friends and neighbors. For men, parish bowling and baseball teams offered a companionable distraction from their work lives. Women cultivated their artistic spirit and enjoyed time away from their families. Laughter and conversation made carrying the burdens of life manageable. It also solidified the Catholic community, as parishioners created their own cultural traditions in an increasingly post-ethnic Utah. Dances and youth activities permitted the young to interact in "safe" environments where they could meet and eventually marry fellow Catholics. Even children played out religious stories to (hopefully) educate, uplift, and entertain. Catholicism is a religion filled with sacred places, holy rituals, inspired leaders, and generous charity. However, without levity and community, religious life is tedious. Love of God and love of neighbor provide the essential ingredients. Leadership sets the structure. The love of fun adds the spice.

One

SACRED SPACES

The photographer who took this mid-1870s panorama of Salt Lake City placed the newly built St. Mary Magdalene Catholic Church prominently at the center, at what would be the intersection of Second East and First South Streets. While there are substantial brick houses nearby, there are no other churches. Across the street are the Wells Fargo Stables and, next door, Feramorz Little's lumberyard. (USHS.)

Utah's first Catholic church was dedicated on November 26, 1871, on property secured by Fr. Edward Kelly in 1866. There were very few Catholics living in Salt Lake City in the 1870s; one account says only 90 souls. Latter-day Saint leader Brigham Young, however, reportedly supported both the church's construction by smoothing over some legal problems and offering money for a school to be built. With the completion of the transcontinental railroad in 1869 and the growth of mining, more "outsiders" were arriving daily. Irish Catholics also made up many of the soldiers stationed at nearby Fort Douglas. Father Kelly arranged for the church to be centrally located, standing a block away from the Salt Lake Theater and across the street from city hall. A substantial redbrick building in a fashionable Gothic design, St. Mary Magdalene's cupola was topped by a gold gilt cross. The church served as the main worship place for Salt Lake Catholics until 1907, when the newly constructed cathedral prompted its closing. The bishop had the deteriorating building demolished in 1917. (USHS.)

Schoolchildren and their teacher stand in front of St. John's Church (founded 1879). The second-oldest Catholic church in the state, it was built in the mining town of Silver Reef. Early Mormon leaders did not approve of the boom-and-bust economy of mining, so many Irish and later Italian Catholics came to settle in isolated mining towns. In August 1873, Archbishop Joseph S. Alemany of San Francisco sent a young Irish priest, Lawrence Scanlan, to minister to the vast lands of Utah Territory. Miners and railroad workers needed to be served in mission stations like Silver Reef, which Scanlan visited in the late 1870s. Priests who eventually ministered in Silver Reef found the town had nine grocery stores, five restaurants, a newspaper, and six saloons. Father Scanlan arranged for the Sisters of the Holy Cross to come to teach Silver Reef children and to nurse in a small hospital. The town did not survive a downturn in silver prices, and the parish complex closed in 1885. A local farmer moved the church building to a nearby town where it served as a social hall for dances, plays, and variety shows. (DSLC.)

While St. Joseph's Parish in Ogden would be founded by Fr. Lawrence Scanlan in 1875, Fr. Patrick M. Cushnahan oversaw the construction of its substantial church. As pastor, Cushnahan ran the parish for almost 50 years. When the parish outgrew its wooden church, he hired Scottish-born architect Francis C. Woods to design a building that spoke to Catholic importance in the city. Despite economic downturns, the church and a rectory were dedicated in 1902. (USHS.)

In 1905, new altars were installed in St. Joseph's Church (above). They reflected Victorian-era Catholicism that connected the faith to its medieval past. A high altar set in front of stained glass, wooden buttresses, and elaborate flanking altars all stressed the drama of the sacrifice of the Mass. Sitting in one of the many wooden pews, Ogden's Catholics might have forgotten for a brief time that they were a minority religious community living among the Latter-day Saints. By 1959, when the boys below posed for their First Holy Communion picture, the war industry had brought more Catholics to the area. Our Lady of Victory Missionary Sisters (Victory Noll Sisters) arrived in 1947 to attend to the religious needs of children not taught in parochial schools. (Both, DSLC.)

When this panorama of Salt Lake City was taken in 1912, the city was a vigorous commercial center. A quarter of the state's population lived in the capital city. Hotels and office buildings dominated the landscape. Rising above the flat-roofed buildings were the twin spires of the newly dedicated St. Mary Magdalene Cathedral. In 1891, Pope Leo III created the Diocese of Salt Lake, a vast territory that included all of Utah and part of eastern Nevada. Fr. Lawrence Scanlan was appointed as first bishop of the new diocese. One of his early goals was to construct a suitable cathedral for the diocese's 5,000 Catholics. (USHS.)

In 1890, Bishop Scanlan purchased lots at South Temple and B Streets to build a new cathedral. Scanlan could imagine a monumental edifice because, in 1899, Mary (Harney) Judge donated $10,000 towards its construction. Mary was the widow of silver magnate John Judge, who had died when he was only 47. Her generosity also funded the cathedral's stained-glass transept windows. The well-regarded city architect, Carl M. Neuhausen, drew up plans for a stately edifice, and more donations poured in from men like Catholic senator Thomas Kearns. The Neo-Romanesque building took several years to complete because Bishop Scanlan refused to go into major debt to fund the church. It was dedicated in 1909 in honor of St. Mary Magdalene. (USHS.)

The cathedral quickly became the focal point of Catholicism in Utah. From families bringing their babies to be baptized to men solemnly burying their compatriots, the church sanctified life from cradle to grave. The cathedral faced one of the main streets of the city, and the holiness of its interior space often spilled out onto its steps. (USHS.)

Bishop Lawrence Scanlan kept an eye on his budget, but his successor Bishop Joseph S. Glass had extravagant taste. From 1915 until his death in 1926, Glass transformed the cathedral's austere interior into a magical space of hand-painted murals, exquisite wood carvings, and fashionable stained-glass windows. Bishop Glass reconstructed the cathedral's front entrance, installing a concrete tympanum above the main portals. He also renamed it the Cathedral of the Madeleine. (USHS.)

In the early years, Utah's Catholics worshipped in spaces they themselves funded, designed, built, and decorated. West of Salt Lake City, in the small town of Tooele, Irish and Italian families had come to work in a smelter that was processing copper and lead. In 1910, they built St. Marguerite's Church with money donated from Tooele banker Frank McGurrin. A successful businessman, McGurrin had won fame and fortune as the world's fastest typist. McGurrin asked that the church be named in honor of his young niece who had recently died. The parishioners hung a bell in their steeple from the old St. Mary Magdalene's in Salt Lake City, the state's first Catholic church. Small lithographs placed in the sanctuary instilled a sacred quality in the simple space. (Both, USHS.)

In the case of Our Divine Savior Church of Salt Lake City, the building had a different life before it became a Catholic church. During the 19th century, Latter-day Saints had conducted extensive missionary work in Scandinavia. Many Swedes arrived in Utah as new converts. Swedish Baptist missionaries came to Salt Lake City in 1891, hoping to convince their fellow countrymen to return to their Protestant faith. Although the Baptists did not make many converts, they did build a church. When their congregation dwindled, the Swedes sold the church in 1918 to the Catholics. Donations of stained glass transformed the modest church into a Catholic sacred space. Even Bishop Joseph Glass provided a gift of an altar rail and baptismal font. In 1950, the parish was renamed to honor the Sacred Heart of Jesus, and a new brick church replaced the old wooden one. The parish now has a large Latinx population, continuing the story of immigrants in the religious life of the city. (USHS.)

Copper ore was discovered in 1848 in the mountains west of Salt Lake City. However, it was not until the end of the 19th century that non-Mormons efficiently and extensively extracted metal ore from an open pit mine located at Bingham Canyon. In 1910, Holy Rosary Church was constructed for the mostly foreign miners. Two years later, the area was the largest mining complex in the world. That same year, a massive strike of 800 men protested the low wages and corrupt practices of mine managers. Mine owners brought in men from Mexico as strikebreakers and some stayed, adding another ethnic group to the Utah Catholic landscape. This photograph from 1926 illustrates how the church was built on the main street right into the side of the mountain (note the steeple at center right). After World War II, it became clear that the mine would engulf the whole town. The church was closed in 1958, and the diocese opened a new parish, dedicated to the Immaculate Heart, in nearby Copperton. (DSLC.)

Coal mining was the economic engine that brought Catholic families to the small town of Helper and the slightly larger town of Price. By the early 1900s, there were 30 mines in the area. Not all Catholic men worked in the mines. French and French Basques came to Price to tend sheep. While the Italian Catholics of Helper in 1914 named their parish St. Antony of Padua, Price's French immigrants in 1923 dedicated their parish to Notre Dame de Lourdes. Bishop Glass had arranged for the Daughters of Charity to teach school in Price at Notre Dame de Lourdes (above), and a Holy Communion class of 1926 proudly posed in front of their church. St. Anthony's in Helper burned to the ground in 1936, but in 1939, despite a worldwide Depression, the families rebuilt their church (below). (Above, USHS; below, DSLC.)

Many counties in Utah are larger than some states. Outside of mining areas, Catholics were few and far between. In 1924, the diocese purchased the house (above) in the small town of Vernal, in the eastern part of the state. Local builders transformed its rooms into spaces for worship (below) and accommodations for a priest, who spent most of his time on the road visiting other mission outposts. At times, the bishop raised funds from Catholic organizations that supported missionary activities. A letter from one of these groups reminded the bishop that their money needed to go to purchase an altar, confessional, altar railing, ostensorium, cope, chalice, ciborium, and Stations of the Cross. (Both, UCL.)

St. Helen's Church in Roosevelt, another rural town, also began in a refurbished house. This photograph from the mid-1950s captures the importance of clerical vestments and popular devotions, like those to Our Lady of Fatima, of the era. Perhaps even more in Mormon Utah, the visible signs of Catholic devotions were critical for cultivating a distinct religious identity. (UCL.)

The Paulist Fathers, an American missionary order, coped with the vastness of the state by bringing "church" to dispersed Catholics. They outfitted a trailer as a "motor chapel." For several summers beginning in 1938, they drove the vehicle throughout the state. A loudspeaker atop the trailer announced their visit. The priests would attract non-Catholics by showing religious movies, like the *King of Kings*. Then they would say Mass and answer questions about their faith. (DSLC.)

Population growth in eastern Utah was stimulated by oil development in nearby Colorado. In 1947, land was purchased in Vernal for a church. The parish's men did the finishing work on the interior, and the church was dedicated to St. James in 1950. It seated 200, and the basement housed a community hall and two kitchens. During the cold months, the parking lot was flooded for ice skating. (UCL.)

After World War II, some Utah mining gave way to skiing. St. Mary of the Assumption Church in Park City was founded by miners in 1882. The town initially flourished from silver mining. However, by 1950, the mines had closed, and the town languished. It would take federal financing in the early 1960s to solidify the ski industry, securing the prosperity of the city. (UU.)

Fire was the great nemesis of mining towns. Because of its placement on a hill, St. Mary's escaped an 1898 fire that decimated the community. It did not, however, avoid a 1950 fire. While Bishop Duane Hunt considered closing the parish, unemployed miners rallied and quickly repaired the church. This 1956 photograph of the choir captures the spirit of a community determined to keep their parish afloat. (DSLC.)

In 1947, an order of contemplative monks established a monastery in Huntsville, Utah. The Cistercians of the Strict Observance (commonly known as the Trappists) practiced a balance of prayer, biblical reading, and work on 1,800 acres of windswept land. They claimed both the space inside their buildings and outside on the landscape as sacred. At its peak in the 1950s, the Abbey of the Holy Trinity housed 80 men who were equally at home herding cattle and mowing hay as they were crafting an intimate relationship with God. The architecture of refurbished Quonset huts spoke to the simplicity of a life focused on the basics of worship and communal life. A general decline in Catholic vocations in the 1970s affected the abbey, and the monks celebrated their last Mass in the monastery in 2017. (Both, DSLC.)

In 1848, Latter-day Saints conducted the first burial in what would become the city cemetery. Catholics, however, required an exclusive space for their dead, and so in 1897, a special section was set aside and named Mount Calvary. This photograph, taken on Memorial Day 1947, shows families remembering the 78 Utah Catholics killed in World War II. (DSLC.)

Even the space under a church can be made "holy" through gestures meant to ensure community safety. In 1962, at the peak of the Cold War, parishioners of St. Joseph's Church in Ogden placed food supplies in the bomb shelter under their church to survive nuclear fallout. (DSLC.)

As a spring celebration to honor the Virgin Mary, May processions often moved outside of the church. A young woman was typically chosen as May queen and given the duty of crowning a statue of the Virgin. In this 1966 photograph, a student from St. Anne's Parish school wears an elaborate wedding dress—evoking both her First Holy Communion and her future wedding day. (DSLC.)

Following the Second Vatican Council (1962–1965), parish churches began to alter their sacred spaces to bring religious life closer to the people. Here, Fr. Louis Fischer introduces the altar boys of St. Anne's Parish to the new design where the priest saying the Mass faces the congregation. Dressed in traditional vestments and with no altar girls, the parish also continued older ritual practices. (DSLC.)

When this First Holy Communion photograph was taken of St. Ambrose Parish children in 1970, gone were the frilly girl's bridal dresses and boys' suits of the past decades. Boys and girls are all dressed alike in simple robes that echo a priest's alb and stole. While the girls still wore simple veils, the robes downplayed gender and class differences. (DSLC.)

In 1776, Catholic priests Francisco Atanazio Dominguez and Silvestre Velez de Escalante entered Utah Valley. Two hundred years later, in 1976, the diocese celebrated both the Catholic presence in Utah and the American bicentennial through a dramatic staged event in the Salt Palace. Over 13,000 Catholics traveled across the state to participate in the event. Representatives from parishes and schools displayed homemade banners during the Mass. State officials, honored guests from other religious communities, and a 100-voice choir joined to acknowledge the long history of Catholics in Utah. (Both, DSLC.)

The 1976 bicentennial celebration also revealed significant changes in Catholic Utah. The Italians and Irish who once dominated Catholic life were now accompanied by immigrants from Vietnam and Mexico. Like earlier Catholics, these men and women also left violence and poverty in their homelands to seek hope and safety in a foreign land. The elaborate priestly vestments that once reflected Victorian elegance gave way to uncomplicated robes that stressed the simplicity of Jesus. Even the massive mural that depicted the momentous expedition of Dominguez and Escalante captured the harsh austerity of lonely exploration rather than the romanticism of colonialism. Still, an altar dominated by men, communion received on the tongue, and a stark crucifix of the suffering Christ linked the present celebration to the Catholic past. (Both, DSLC.)

Educating the mind, body, and soul of Catholic youth was a central mission of the church in Utah. Although the exact date of this photograph is unknown, by the early 20th century, St. Mary's Academy for girls was thriving. In 1916, twenty-six professed sisters and five novices taught 89 boarding students and 182 day students. Their school building was substantial and well-equipped. Both Catholic and non-Catholic girls benefited from the talents of teaching sisters. (DSLC.)

Two

EDUCATING

In 1873, when Fr. (later bishop) Lawrence Scanlan arrived in Salt Lake City, he had two goals: to free the existing church from debt and to establish a school. Within two years, Scanlan arranged for two Sisters of the Holy Cross to open a private academy for girls. Catholic education was critical if the church was to survive within a community dominated economically, politically, and culturally by the Latter-day Saints. (SCH.)

Even non-Catholics valued "convent" education for girls. Consequently, the Sisters of the Holy Cross had no difficulty filling the seats of St. Mary's Academy. In the 1870s, there were only about 10 Catholic families in the city, but over 150 girls were being educated by the sisters. Within the decade, that number increased to 200. By the time that this picture was taken in the 1910s, three hundred girls were enrolled. An estimated one-third of the student body was not Catholic. Girls studied the "three Rs" (reading, writing, and arithmetic), ancient and modern languages, and religion. Older girls were exposed to botany, chemistry, and even astronomy. Art and music classes were also offered. By 1890, bookkeeping, shorthand, and typewriting could be taken as a part of a commercial course of study. If this young woman graduate did not want a secretarial career, she could accept automatic admission to the University of Utah where she would enter as a sophomore. Or she might have pursued marriage—assured that her poise, purity, and gracefulness would merit her a good match. (DSLC.)

Unlike later in the century when Catholic schooling was almost equated with the word "uniform," the girls of St. Mary's came to school in fashionable attire (above). The sisters ensured that their dress was clean, modest, and efficient. In addition to cultivating feminine values, St. Mary's upheld the civic virtues of early-20th-century America. In the below photograph, clergy and students raise a flag during what might have been a spring festival to honor the Virgin Mary. Patriotism and Catholicism were both understood to be essential virtues of a true woman. (Both, DSLC.)

In 1908, the girls of St. Mary's enjoyed tennis and basketball on their spacious playground. Being fit and coordinated was a part of the "physical culture" craze of the early 20th century. By the next decade, girls were taking archery, fencing, and even military marching. Their schoolyard was shaded by trees probably planted when the academy was founded in 1875. (USHS.)

The instructors at St. Mary's Academy, like Sister Rita (Louise Heffernan), made sure that the girls cultivated a balanced life of intellectual engagement, religious devotion, patriotic commitment, and feminine propriety. Sister Rita had also attended St. Mary's Academy in the 1870s when her family moved to Salt Lake City. After her time teaching at St. Mary's, Sister Rita would go on to do graduate studies at Harvard University and then teach at the order's motherhouse college in Indiana. (SCH.)

St. Mary's Academy students attended Mass in an elaborately designed chapel. These photographs from 1909 capture the exuberance of Victorian Catholicism. From the stenciling on the walls to the colorful statues to the proliferation of plants and flowers, the goal was to make worship a sensual experience. Even newfangled electric lightbulbs caused a halo to glow across the niches where statues of the Virgin Mary and St. Joseph stood. When one of the students died (below), the community came together to mourn their loss. Black crepe draped on the altar reminded them of their sorrow, while the white banner and coffin symbolized the innocence of youth and the glory of heavenly life. Death was not hidden away but presented as an expected, but difficult, aspect of the natural order. (Above, DSLC; below, USHS.)

All Hallows College for boys opened in 1886 at Fourth East and Second South Streets. Fr. Lawrence Scanlan named the school after his own alma mater in Dublin, Ireland. As a "preparatory college," the school was a combination of a high school and junior college. In 1889, Father Scanlan secured the service of the Fathers of the Society of Mary (Marists) to teach the young men. The Marists offered a varied curriculum of three programs: classical, scientific, and commercial. In addition to a band that may have played at their extensive sporting events, All Hallows College also boasted an orchestra. There also was a military flare to the school as students wore uniforms and were called "cadets." At its peak, the school taught between 180 and 200 students, with twice as many boarders as day students. During a time when Catholic education in the West was rare, All Hallows College drew students from the nearby states and as far away as California. (USHS.)

All Hallows College initially flourished. A new wing with a chapel was added in 1903 that linked together the two school buildings (above). However, by 1910, when this portrait of the Marist faculty and administration was taken, student numbers had begun to decline (below). The local community was less eager to pay to educate their boys than they were their girls because young men were needed on farms and in businesses. In addition, Bishop Scanlan was in a power struggle with the Marists and eventually pulled all diocesan support from the school. In 1918, the Marist Fathers admitted that All Hallows College was incapable of supporting itself. The order withdrew from the diocese, and the school closed. (Both, USHS.)

40

All Hallows College, like most boys' schools of the time, was committed to sports as an avenue to build manly men. The college mustered both football and baseball teams. Their head coach, John Frederick Tobin, sits on the top row, center. Team sports built comradeship, cultivated physical agility, and promoted acceptable forms of competition. Sports even served to temper lustful passion. It was thought that through sports like football, the male tendency toward violence could be channeled into appropriate avenues like military nationalism. Catholics were often seen as outsiders to the American Protestant culture or, in Utah, Mormon society. Consequently, sports also provided a way for Catholic men to "fit in." (USHS.)

The Sisters of the Holy Cross established Sacred Heart Academy in 1878 in Ogden. The school survived in this renovated house until 1892. At that point, increased enrollment necessitated a new academy on a five-acre lot at Twenty-fifth Street between Quincy and Jackson Avenues. As in other parts of the state, non-Catholics were taught as well as Catholics. In 1927, for instance, there were 30 Catholic and 36 non-Catholic boarding students as well as 93 Catholic and 88 non-Catholic day pupils. During that year, four students converted and were baptized into the faith. (DSLC.)

In 1882, the Sisters of the Holy Cross started teaching students at St. Mary's of the Assumption Church in Park City. By the 1890s, under the direction of two enthusiastic priests, Fathers Patrick Blake and Thomas Galligan, the school had almost 200 pupils. This photograph from 1910 gives a sense of the crowding of the classrooms. Unlike the academies that charged tuition, at this point in Catholic history parish schools were free. The sisters did charge extra for training in instrumental music, voice, and piano. They even taught guitar and mandolin. (DSLC.)

By the 1920s, St. Mary's Academy was outgrowing its now old building in Salt Lake City. In 1921, the Sisters of the Holy Cross purchased a large tract of land on the outskirts of town. They opened St. Mary of the Wasatch College and Academy for Women in 1926. In addition to a full liberal arts program, the college offered a pre-nursing curriculum taught in cooperation with Holy Cross Hospital. Classrooms and a library were accompanied by tennis courts, a gymnasium, and a social hall. The interior was filled with heavy wood carved paneling, marble floors, and elaborate rosewood and velvet furniture. The sisters installed a six-ton bell that tolled at noon and 6:00 p.m. so all would know when to stop and pray the Angelus. (SCH.)

When St. Mary of the Wasatch College opened at Thirteenth South and Thirtieth East, its buildings stood on 400 acres of barren land. To transport students, the sisters arranged for buses (above) to travel on unpaved roads. The entrance to the school was marked by a stone gate and tower, which is all that remains now of the educational complex (below). (Both, SCH.)

St. Mary of the Wasatch College graduates from 1927 sit proudly with Bishop John Joseph Mitty, looking forward to an uncertain future (above). Following World War I, more women were experiencing changes in how they lived their lives. Relations between men and women became more relaxed. Clothing softened, and hemlines rose. More single women were working before marriage. Catholic education, however, continued to stress feminine refinement illustrated by this 1920 photograph of harpists from St. Mary's performing at the recently opened Pantages Theatre (below). (Above, DSLC; below, USHS.)

While St. Mary of the Wasatch College and Academy survived the economic hardships of the Great Depression, cultural changes after World War II caused a downturn in enrollment. Coeducation became even more popular, and the Victorian flourishes of St. Mary's did not match well with the new "teen" culture of postwar America. Public high schools now provided suitable education for girls, who in the 1950s were being told to marry early and focus exclusively on family life. St. Mary of the Wasatch College closed in 1970, and the buildings were eventually demolished. (DSLC.)

Judge Memorial High School began its life as John Judge Memorial Home, a miner's hospital. It was transformed in 1920 into an elementary school staffed by the Daughters of Charity of St. Vincent de Paul. High school grades were added, and in 1923, the Sisters of the Holy Cross took over the teaching of the older students in what was known as Cathedral High School. (USHS.)

In 1929, Bishop Joseph John Mitty changed the name of the school to Judge Memorial High School to recognize the importance of the Judge family to Catholic Utah. In 1867, Mary Harney married John Judge, who would make a fortune in silver mining. When he died at 48, Mary (Harney) Judge astutely managed the family's money by investing in mines and real estate. In addition to funding the hospital, she was a committed donor to the cathedral. She died in 1909. (DSLC.)

By the late 1950s, it was clear that a former hospital no longer could serve as a high school for a growing Salt Lake City. The city's Catholics worked hard to raise money, and parishes were encouraged to see the new high school as their own (above). A new Judge Memorial building was constructed next to the old structure on 1100 East and dedicated on November 6, 1960. For a short time, from 1964 to 1970, the Oblates of St. Francis de Sales operated the high school exclusively for boys, but when St. Mary of the Wasatch College closed, the school resumed its coeducational status. In this undated photograph of the football team, two unidentified priests stand proudly next to Bishop Duane Hunt and the youthful players (below). (Both, DSLC.)

In 1944, the Sisters of the Holy Cross started a summer school in the area of Vernal. In this 1953 photograph (above), their religion classes at St. James Church used modern teaching methods to engage the children. During the 1940s, the Our Lady of Victory Missionary Sisters had come to Utah (below). Unlike other orders who staffed schools, these sisters (also known as the Victory Noll Sisters) provided Catholic instructions in remote areas that could not support parochial schools. They moved from place to place as the need demanded. The children seem pleased with their summer school curriculum. (Both, UCL.)

In these photographs from 1955, Franciscan Sisters of the Atonement and St. Helen's Parish priest are shown transporting (above) and teaching children (below) at their religious summer school. St. Helen's had a large Native population because, during the 19th century, some of the Indigenous people of Utah were forced onto a reservation in the northeast section of the state near Roosevelt. Then, that land was taken and distributed, with much of it landing in non-Native hands. Some of the Native children identified above are, in the first row, third from left, Forrest Cuch (Ute); next to him, Michael Arrowchis (Ute); second from right, and Tex Smiley Arrowchis (Ute). Of the shorter girls standing on the second row, fourth from left is Roberta Johnson (Ute/Assiniboine). On the back row standing third from left is LaFern Caudell (Bannock/Choctaw); to her right, Patricia Johnson (Ute/Assiniboine); and fifth from left, Lea LaRose (Shoshone/Bannock). (Both, UCL.)

An important aspect of Catholic life in the mid-20th century was the parochial school. Education did not simply engage children; the whole family was expected to support the schools. In this 1963 photograph, the men of St. Joseph's Parish in Ogden paint one of the classrooms in the school. (DSLC.)

Postwar population growth meant more children in parochial schools. When this photograph was taken in 1966, the number of women religious in the United States was at its peak. The Sisters of the Holy Cross—many of them young and enthusiastic—staffed the Cathedral School begun in 1949. The sisters organized an after-school Savio Club, named after the child saint Dominic Savio (1842–1857), who was canonized in 1954. (DSLC.)

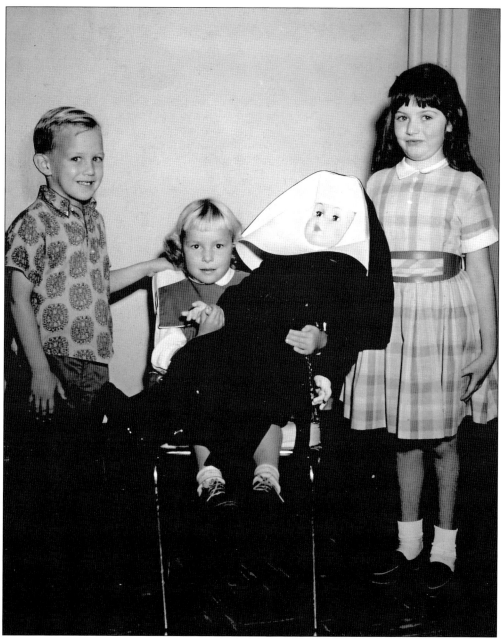

Parochial schools were critical in encouraging Catholic vocations to the sisterhood and priesthood. Children watched their teachers, and some were inspired to devote their lives to the church. In the early 1960s, three Salt Lake City children from St. Ann's school were photographed holding a large doll wearing the habit of their teachers: the Sisters of Charity of the Incarnate Word. (DSLC.)

To keep children engaged and to stimulate friendly competition, contests were held with prizes given out. In 1965, Sister Mary Ernestine, a teacher at St. Ann's school, hands Mary Kathleen Cook her gift for winning a contest during Student Health Week. A statue of Our Lady of Fatima stands in a prominent place reminding viewers of the link between Catholic education, religious commitment, and the supernatural. (DSLC.)

There had been a Catholic presence in Provo since 1892, and Franciscan priests had come in 1931. St. Francis of Assisi school was established in 1955, and when this picture was taken in 1960, it proudly transported elementary children by school bus. The school closed in 1971 when the Franciscan Sisters of Perpetual Adoration decided that there were no longer enough sisters in their community to sufficiently staff the school. (DSLC.)

These Franciscan Sisters of the Atonement from St. James Church in Vernal were photographed in 1968 wearing their new, "modified" habit. The Second Vatican Council (1962–1965) had asked sisters to return to their order's original mission and evaluate whether their habits were supportive of those goals. Many orders of women religious simplified their habits to make them more practical for executing their responsibilities. (UCL.)

Critical to the Catholic mission in Utah (and across the globe) was to provide healing to those who were sick. This healing assumed an intertwining of the physical body of the person and their spiritual soul: to care for one meant to care for the other. In addition, the New Testament tells of the many miracles Jesus performed to heal the sick and disabled. Catholics who sought to follow Christ often embraced his call to heal as evidence of their religious commitments. By the mid-20th century, when this photograph was taken, the Sisters of the Holy Cross ran a modern hospital and a fully accredited school of nursing. (DSLC.)

Three

HEALING

In 1875, the Sisters of the Holy Cross responded to a call from Fr. Lawrence Scanlan to begin a hospital in Salt Lake City. When this photograph was taken around 1883, the sisters had built a sophisticated medical institution on a 10-acre block between Tenth and Eleventh East on 100 South. By 1891, seventeen sisters worked in the hospital. (SCH.)

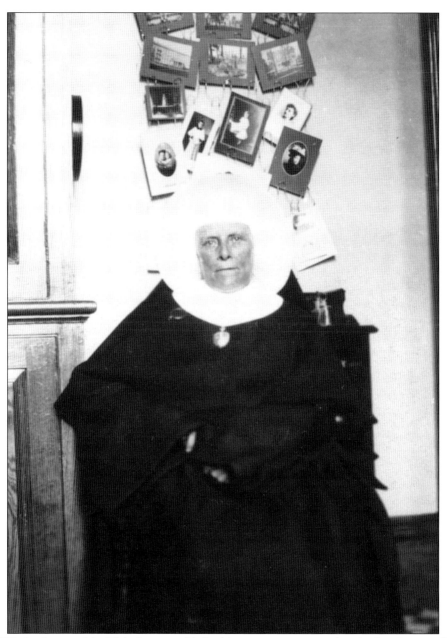

In 1887, the Sisters of the Holy Cross established St. Lawrence Hospital in Ogden. Sister Lidwina (birth name Annette Butler), along with Sister Philip and Sister Valentina, rented a building where they cared for employees of the Union Pacific and, later, the Southern Pacific Railroads. Eventually, a new building was erected near the old one. Unlike in other aspects of American society where men controlled important institutions, the Holy Cross Mother Superior ran every aspect of hospital life—including hiring and firing male doctors. The sisters negotiated with the railroad companies to financially support their employees who were often injured at work. Union Pacific provided the building, medicine, and surgical supplies along with a $5 fee for each worker for whom the sisters cared. When a city hospital was built, the companies no longer supported St. Lawrence, and the hospital closed in 1898. (SCH.)

The sisters named their hospital in Salt Lake City as St. Mary's Hospital of the Holy Cross. It soon became shortened to Holy Cross Hospital. Latter-day Saint women had also opened a hospital, but Holy Cross became the preferred medical establishment of the city. By the late 1880s, when this photograph was taken, caring for the sick in hospitals was replacing caring for them in homes. Holy Cross Hospital contained 125 beds and, during its first year, served 450 patients. The sisters had constructed a three-story brick building that housed a luxurious hall, a spacious auditorium, and a series of elegantly furnished private rooms. Special wards were designated for women, for people with typhoid, for convalescents, and for surgical patients. In 1892, the staff oversaw the care of almost 1,000 patients per year. Given that in 1890 there were only 8,000 Catholics living in Utah and Nevada compared to a total Utah population of 207,905, it was clear that Mormon and non-Mormon alike preferred to be healed in a Catholic space. (SCH.)

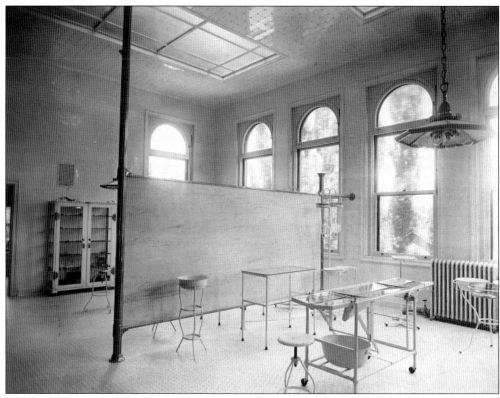

While Catholic sisters did not become doctors until the 20th century, they did make sure that their hospitals had the most up-to-date examining rooms (above) and surgical rooms (below). The Sisters of the Holy Cross initiated an "open staffing" policy that permitted as many reputable physicians as possible to have admitting privileges at Holy Cross Hospital. Those doctors brought in paying patients whose dollars enabled the purchasing of modern equipment and the expansion of the hospital. (USHS.)

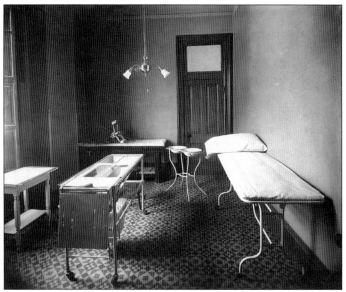

When these photographs were taken in 1904 (above) and 1908 (left), Holy Cross Hospital had a new steam plant to supply its own heat and power, a greenhouse, and even an elevator system. (USHS.)

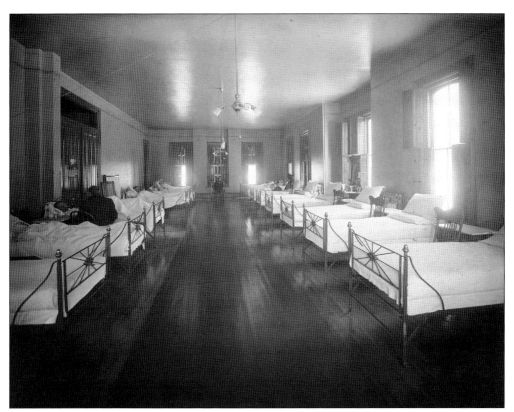

The Sisters of the Holy Cross created a healing space that was adapted to the financial needs of different types of patients. In this 1908 photograph of a ward (above), cleanliness, orderliness, and efficiency are stressed. Neatly made beds are ready for those who could not afford private rooms. (USHS.)

On the other hand, a private room (right) from the same year is elegantly furnished. Floral carpet, a dresser, and a framed picture of the Madonna and child transform a medical space into a comfortable bedroom. Such rooms even had electric call bells to summon staff. (USHS.)

A critical difference between healing at home and healing in a hospital was the ability of the staff to prescribe and effectively dispense an array of medicines. Like in contemporary hospitals, this 1908 pharmacy at Holy Cross Hospital stored chemicals and compounds. Such medicines were believed to be scientifically proven to cure disease and ease pain. The photographer captured both the proliferation of pills and elixirs that spoke to the modern character of medicine as well as the physical beauty of the tile floor and wooden cabinetry. (USHS.)

As with all Catholic institutions, no space would be complete without a chapel where Mass could be offered. Especially in a hospital where the sick faced suffering and death, having a place for prayer and rituals was essential. The chapel most clearly represented the Catholic understanding of the unification of the spiritual soul with the physical body. Holy Cross Chapel was designed by Carl M. Neuhausen, the architect of Salt Lake's Cathedral of the Madeleine. This 1904 interior photograph shows some of the chapel's 11 stained-glass windows and marble altarpieces. The chapel has been consistently renovated. In 1909, Achille Peretti from New Orleans was brought in to paint gold-leaf designs on the sanctuary ceiling and frescoes on the walls. In 1915, a grandfather clock was added. Although the Stations of the Cross and elaborate altars would be removed under the simplifying impulse of the Second Vatican Council, the beauty of the chapel continues into the 21st century. (USHS.)

Holy Cross School of Nursing was founded in 1901 and offered single women a reputable profession that combined maternal care with scientific exactitude and Christian compassion. These students sat for a class portrait around 1910. While their dress recalls that of tidy house servants, they understood nursing as an avenue to independence. Female nursing students, like those who attended the girls' academies run by the Sisters of the Holy Cross, did not have to be Catholic. Indeed, the only individual identified in this photograph is Hannah Claire Haines (back row, third from the right), a non-Catholic who would later leave nursing to become the first female certified public accountant in Utah. Haines would eventually become the director of a Salt Lake City bank. Holy Cross School of Nursing closed in 1973. (WC.)

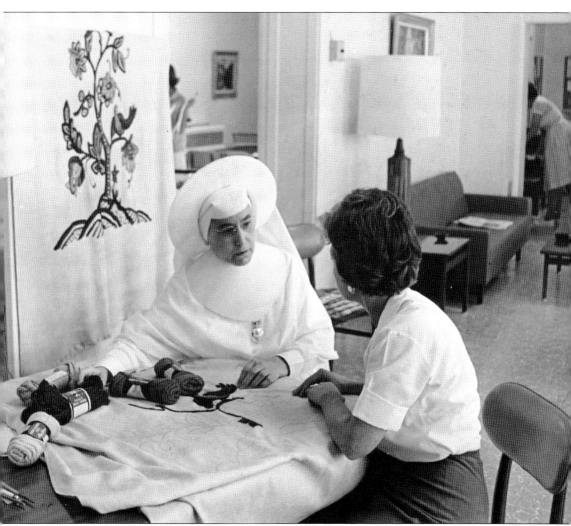

By 1964, when this photograph was taken, the Sisters of the Holy Cross ran a sophisticated hospital in the heart of Salt Lake City. Not only did they assist in operating rooms, care for medical patients, and teach student nurses, they offered rehabilitation services to recovering patients. Here, Sister M. Laurent provides occupational therapy in a homelike environment. (SHC.)

To provide medical care to a growing population, the Benedictine Sisters started a hospital in Ogden. Sr. Mary Margaret Clifford (left) and Sr. Estelle Nordick (right) stand at the doors of St. Benedict Hospital at its opening in 1946. During World War II and immediately after, Utah became an important center of the defense industry. Soldiers and factory workers settled in Ogden, in the northern part of the state. (SSB.)

Taken on the day of its dedication in 1946, St. Benedict Hospital stands assertively in front of the Wasatch range of mountains in this image. Hospital care in Ogden had been unstable until the influx of defense workers required more consistent care. A city hospital had briefly existed, and an influential local businessman, Thomas D. Dee, had built a medical facility that was eventually taken over by the Church of Jesus Christ of Latter-day Saints. The expansion of military installations in the area, however, drew in workers from out of state. In 1940, the War Department announced it would support the construction of a new hospital rather than renovate the old Dee hospital. Since the city did not have the funds to staff a new facility, civic leaders approached the pastor of Ogden's St. Joseph's Church, Msgr. Wilfrid J. Giroux. They hoped he might be able to secure the commitments of an order of hospital sisters. (DSLC.)

Mass is said on the steps of St. Benedict Hospital in Ogden at its dedication on September 19, 1946. According to a story told about the hospital, Msgr. Wilfrid J. Giroux was not sure how to go about building a medical center. So, he opened the *Catholic Directory*, which included a list of names of religious orders of women. Starting in alphabetical order, he soon found a Benedictine community with over 1,200 sisters who managed hospitals as a part of their mission. Monsignor Giroux decided that if they had that many sisters, surely, they could spare a few for this Mormon territory. He wrote Mother Rosamond Pratschner of St. Benedict's priory in St. Joseph, Minnesota, describing his needs. While Mother Rosamond did not have any plans to send sisters to the West, she did write back that his project seemed interesting. Within a week, Monsignor Giroux was ringing the doorbell of the Minnesota motherhouse explaining to the amused Mother Rosamond, "I came to get my sisters." (USHS.)

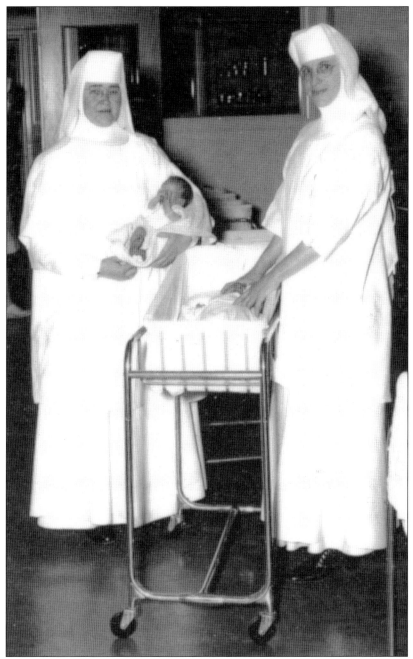

Sr. Estelle Nordick (left) and Sr. Mary Margaret Clifford (right) care for newborn infants at St. Benedict Hospital in Ogden. Funds to create a modern hospital came from large organizations like the National Board for Infantile Paralysis and the local community, which included the Ogden Community Chest and St. Joseph's Parish. While the Benedictines provided direct medical care along with lay nurses, doctors, and staff, they also were the hospital's administrators and business managers. Their insights into the expanding American health care system kept St. Benedict's at the cutting edge of medicine. In 1946, for instance, the area's first orthopedic surgeon joined the staff. In 1949, a psychiatric unit was added and, a year later, a social service department. (SSB.)

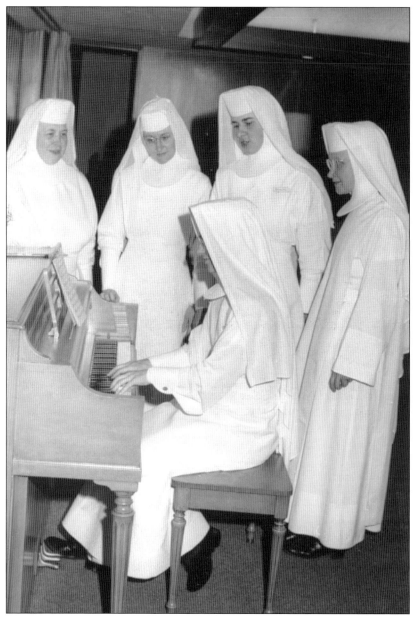

Taking a break from their medical responsibilities, sisters at St. Benedict's Hospital enjoy a musical interlude in their convent. They are, from left to right, sisters Nivelle Berning, Elizabeth Maher, Pacelli Zensen, Merle Maerz, and Danile Knight (at piano). In the postwar years, when this photograph was taken, the Benedictine Sisters were an anomaly in Mormon Utah. While their white habits dominated their hospital lives, they would change to black ones to go downtown. There, the pairs of sisters would elicit the stares of their Mormon neighbors unused to seeing such elaborate outfits. Sisters recalled that they even frightened some children. Non-Catholic hospital staff voiced concerns that, because they were unmarried women, the sisters would never gain earthly happiness or merit eternal salvation. Still, both the sisters and the local clergy believed that hospital work was a perfect avenue for indirect missionary work. Their flowing habits as well as their loving care in the hospital provoked conversations and questions that could lead in many directions. (SSB.)

St. Benedict's School of Nursing opened in April 1947, and this portrait is of the class of 1948. Sisters, trained at some of the nation's best hospitals, went on to teach Utah women to be nurses. (USHS.)

Sisters at the St. Benedict's School of Nursing ran a three-year, hospital-based program. Students lived near the hospital in a nurses' building that accommodated 110 women (no men were accepted then). As with other aspects of hospital life, as the nature of nursing changed so did St. Benedict's School. Nursing education was moving out of hospitals and into colleges. In 1966, St. Benedict's School associated with a local college, and the Weber State College Practical Nurse program was born. The last class trained at St. Benedict's graduated in 1968. (WSU.)

The "capping ceremony" of St. Benedict Hospital nursing students was dramatic and meaningful. Above, Sister Beno initiates a graduate in 1951. Another woman watches, dressed as the famous nurse Florence Nightingale. Below, a 1965 *Intermountain Catholic* article explained that the candle symbolized the nurse's role to carry Christ to all as he was the "Light of the World." The cape signified loyalty and love, while the nursing cap symbolized healing. The candles, caps, and capes were blessed by Msgr. Patrick F. Kennedy. Fr. Thomas Dove, from St. Rose of Lima Church in nearby Layton, acted as master of ceremonies. (Both, DSLC.)

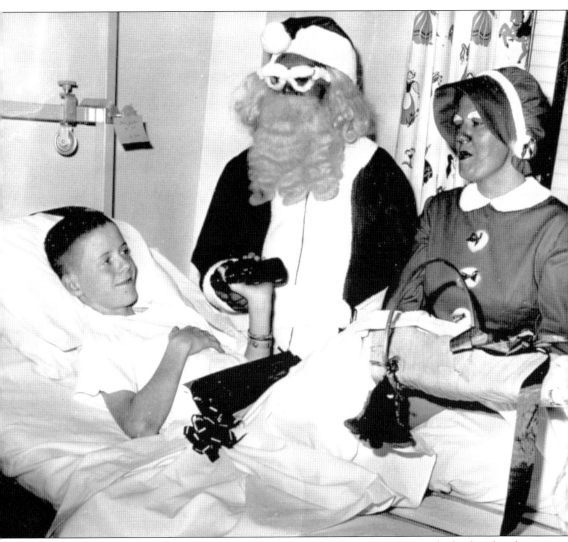

Laymen and laywomen, in addition to being doctors, nurses, and staff at St. Benedict's, also played a critical role in creating a community-based hospital. In 1963, an *Intermountain Catholic* photographer captured Santa and Mrs. Santa Claus visiting a patient in a pediatric ward. Although typically a space of pain and discomfort, some individuals found time to bring cheerful goofiness to the sick and injured. The child patient looks somewhat dubious, but for the adults, the performance embodied their commitment to Christian charity. Dressing in silly clothing and visiting during the Christmas season permitted non-employees of St. Benedict's to claim that the hospital, at least on some level, belonged to them. (DSLC.)

Throughout Catholic history, laymen and laywomen funneled needed resources into hospitals. No hospital could survive without income coming in from community donations. Here, a nursing sister from St. Benedict's Hospital, Ogden, chats with two volunteers as they plan and make decorations for a fundraising luncheon. Photographed in the early 1960s, it evokes an era when middle-class women, who were not preoccupied with wage labor, directed their energies towards churches, schools, and civic organizations. Unpaid volunteer work provided creative outlets and spaces for socializing while addressing pressing needs. During a time when Catholic sisters lived isolated in their own communities, charitable activities provided a rare opportunity to enjoy the company of other women. (DSLC.)

By 1964, when women were organizing this Spring Charity Ball for Holy Cross Hospital, change was in the air. Betty Friedan had just published *The Feminine Mystique*, which gave voice to women's frustrations with their limited gender roles. In addition, the Second Vatican Council was reforming the place of the laity within the church and encouraging their more direct involvement with the spiritual life of the parish. Women began to see themselves not simply as fundraisers. The Catholic medical world would eventually feel the impact of these social and religious changes. (DSLC.)

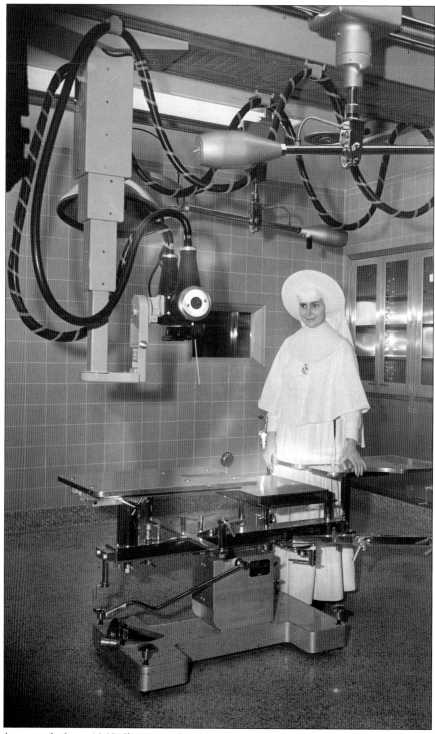

This photograph from 1960 illustrates the discontinuity between the traditional Sisters of the Holy Cross habit and the equipment used in modern health care. Increasingly, hospital care was becoming more technological and expensive. (USHS.)

Holy Cross Hospital in Salt Lake City would expand throughout the 1950s and 1960s. However, by the 1970s, the number of women entering religious orders was rapidly declining. Hospital care also required an increasingly large staff who were professionally trained and paid commensurate salaries. New services and buildings placed financial and managerial strain on the orders that ran Catholic hospitals in Salt Lake City and Ogden. (HC.)

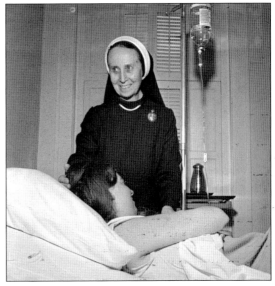

Sister M. Ann Josephine in 1968 wears the modified habit of the Sisters of the Holy Cross. To maintain a Catholic medical presence in Ogden, the Benedictines negotiated in 1986 a joint sponsorship with Holy Cross Health System. However, in 1994, the Sisters of the Holy Cross completed the sale of all their hospitals in Utah to a non-Catholic, for-profit hospital corporation. Then in 2023, the hospital became a part of CommonSpirit Health, a national, nonprofit, Catholic health system. (USHS.)

This unidentified photograph was probably taken between 1930 and 1940. It shows Ute Indian women and girls with two Catholic sisters. (UCL.)

Four

CARING

Kearns-St. Ann's Orphanage was established in 1891. By 1900, a major edifice had been constructed. While some children had parents no longer living, many more had parents who were too poor to care for them. (USHS.)

The original orphanage at Third East and First South soon became too small to house the city's poor children. Mining, which increasingly brought Catholics to Utah, was a dangerous industry with families suffering from the deaths and illnesses of their breadwinners. Parishes held fairs and bazaars to raise money for a new building. Then in 1899, mining magnate Thomas Kearns gave $50,000 to enable Bishop Lawrence Scanlan to purchase property located on what is now 2100 South Street and 500 East Street. At that time, the building was on the outskirts of the city so the Sisters of the Holy Cross who cared for the children also raised much of their food. The building was designed by Carl M. Neuhausen, who also was the architect of the Cathedral of the Madeleine. On May 1, 1900, shortly before the new building opened, 200 miners were killed in the Utah mountains when coal dust ignited with explosive force. Bishop Scanlan wrote in the diocesan newspaper that the new orphanage would welcome and comfort all the children from those families who needed care. (DSLC.)

Thomas Kearns (second row, left) came to Park City as a young man in 1883 to seek his fortune in mining. In 1889, he and a partner discovered a rich vein of ore that became the Silver King Coalition mine. A year later, he married another Catholic, Jennie Judge (first row, left). Their surviving children were Helen (second row, center), Edmond (second row, right), and Tom (first row, right). Thomas Kearns would develop other mines in Colorado, Nevada, and California, becoming one of the wealthiest men in Utah. He served in the US Senate from 1901 to 1905, and his elaborately designed home would become the official residence of the governor. (USHS.)

Most likely, this undated portrait is of the Sisters of the Holy Cross who cared for orphans at Kearns-St. Ann's. Caring for orphans, in addition to teaching and nursing, was an essential part of the sisters' ministry. Since the order's establishment in 1840, the women had directed orphanages in Indiana, Michigan, Louisiana (Marianites of Holy Cross), Maryland, and Washington, DC. The sisters housed, fed, and clothed children of any religion whose parents had died, abandoned them, or were unable to care for them. Within a few months of its opening in 1900, the sisters cared for approximately 92 children. The goal of the orphanage was to educate and train the children so they could find employment and become self-sufficient. (SHC.)

These undated photographs, probably from the 1940s, stress the happy domestic life of the orphaned children. Like other children, they had their faces washed (above), played with dolls, and made their own beds. National standards of child welfare, however, had changed. Federal and state funding for dependent children as well as foster care were replacing orphanages. In 1953, the Sisters of the Holy Cross left Kearns-St. Ann's Orphanage. The Sisters of Charity of the Incarnate Word continued it for a year, and then the director of Catholic Charities for the diocese permanently closed the facility. St. Ann's Parish school opened in the same building in 1955. (Both, DSLC.)

This 1952 portrait of First Holy Communion Day at St. Helen's in Roosevelt shows children looking happy and thriving. This had not always been the case with Utah's Indigenous people. During the 19th century, diverse groups of Native people who had survived illness, warfare, and poverty were pushed to the eastern part of Utah. By 1882, the Uintah, White River, and Uncompahgre Utes were forced to live on the dry land of the Uintah reservation. The federal government then allotted land to individuals and dissolved most of the reservation, a move rejected by the Utes. In 1905, lands were opened to white homesteading. Ed Harmston turned his homestead claim into a townsite, naming it Roosevelt after the president. His wife, Mary, deeded land to the diocese, and in 1940, St. Helen's church/house was built. During the 1930s, the government changed some of its attitudes towards Native people, increasing the reservation size. Then in the 1950s, the Utes won multiple legal battles that awarded $32 million in settlements. Half of that went to Utah bands, spurring economic development and stabilizing families. (UCL.)

Caring for children in the remote parts of Utah included preparing them for their First Holy Communion. In 1952, Victory Noll Sisters brought together all the Catholic children from the area to help them learn the meaning of the Eucharist. For the special Mass, girls wore fancy dresses, and boys donned dress shirts. Afterward, the families shared a meal together. This Ute child poses for one of the many photographs taken that day, which celebrated the parish's children. (UCL.)

In 1947, Bishop Duane G. Hunt invited the Sisters of Charity of the Incarnate Word to open a home for the elderly. The sisters bought a mansion built in the 1890s by a mining magnate and named it St. Joseph's Villa (above). In addition to housing the frail aged, St. Joseph's Villa provided retirement accommodations for diocesan priests. In 1959, the mansion was torn down, and a modern nursing home was constructed (below). (Both, DSLC.)

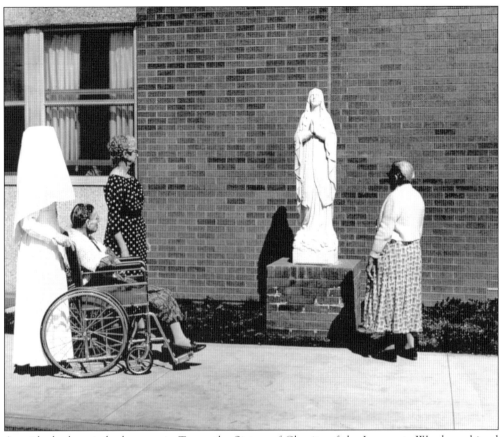

As with the hospitals they ran in Texas, the Sisters of Charity of the Incarnate Word combined charitable service and Catholic sensibility with modern efficiency. Above, a sister wheels a resident to a statue of Our Lady of Lourdes while two other women look on. Below, a sister demonstrates the telephone system of the newly opened facility. (Both, DSLC.)

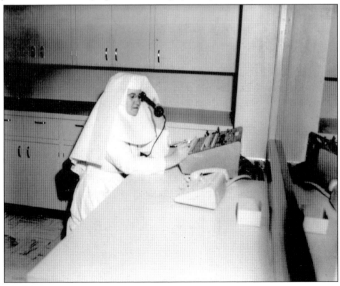

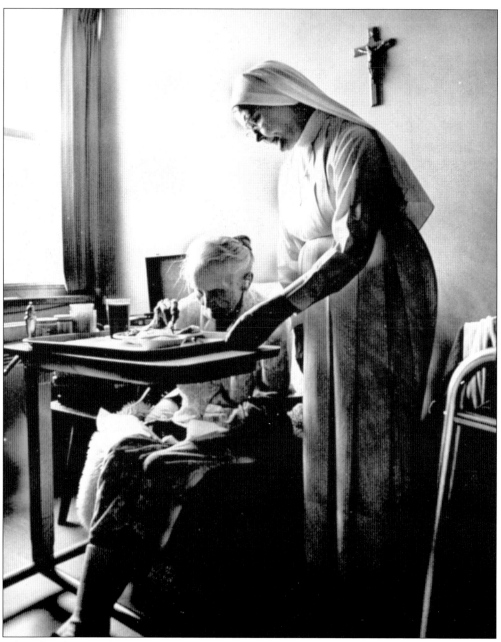

When this photograph was taken in 1974, the Sisters of Charity of the Incarnate Word were wearing modified habits. Although their numbers would dwindle, they continued to manage St. Joseph's Villa nursing home until 2011 when it was sold to a for-profit, post-acute care company. (DSLC.)

This photograph from the early 1970s shows a religious education class of deaf students. While Catholics only made up a small portion of the students at the Utah School for the Deaf and Blind in Ogden, they did not neglect their faith. Sr. Carolyn Lopez (standing left) and Sister Wallsteadt (standing right) instruct in sign language at their convent to enable the students to deepen their understanding of their religion. The sisters no longer wore religious habits. Victory Noll Sisters had been in Ogden since 1947 and in Salt Lake City since 1939. Their ministry focused on caring for people not addressed through typical Catholic parishes and schools. They taught religious education at various state-supported schools and rural parishes. The sisters also supported the poor and ministered to the sick and elderly. (DSLC.)

Victory Noll Sisters also coordinated religious education classes at the federally run Intermountain Indian School, founded in 1950. The sisters arrived in 1951 and taught weekly classes to mostly Navajo teenagers. In these photographs from 1965, Mrs. Peak, a Confraternity of Christian Doctrine teacher (above), and Sister Mary Beatrice (below) instruct a class of mostly young women. (Both, DSLC.)

In 1965, when these pictures were taken, 2,000 Navajo students between ages 12 and 21 studied at the school. Here, Sister Kateri and several students arrive at religion classes. The Intermountain Indian School served Navajo children mostly bussed from Arizona and New Mexico. It was the largest off-reservation boarding school for Navajo students. Children would spend nine months out of the year studying in Utah and then return to their homes in the summer. In the 1970s, after an expansion, the school taught children from over 100 tribes. (DSLC.)

A smiling Sister Mary Beatrice is photographed in 1965 meeting with students at the Intermountain Indian School. During the summer, some of the sisters lived with their Navajo students so they could learn more about their cultures. Victory Noll Sisters (also known as the Missionary Catechists of Our Lady of Victory) were a relatively new religious order. Founded in 1922 by Fr. John Joseph Sigstein, the order sought to minister to remote communities underserved by the church. Sigstein wanted the women not to be hampered by elaborate habits, and so they wore "uniforms," without a veil that totally covered their hair or a rosary. The first sisters were sent to New Mexico. There, as in Utah, sisters provided religious education in small towns with no parochial schools. The sisters prepared students for baptism, first communion, and confirmation. (DSLC.)

Sister Anna, one of the Victory Noll Sisters, offers advice during a chess game to students from the Intermountain Indian School (above). Students were taken to St. Henry's parish in Brigham City for Sunday Mass, after which they enjoyed relaxing with each other and the sisters. Bishop Joseph Lennox Federal is shown in 1964 confirming Native students in the Intermountain Indian School auditorium (below). (Both, DSLC.)

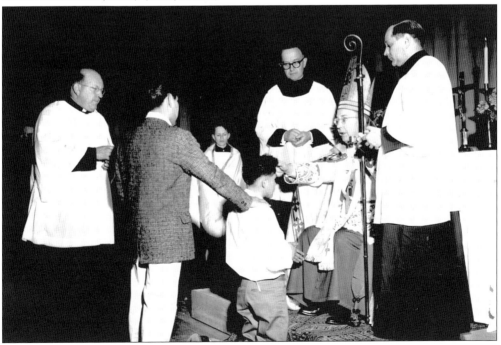

Typically, in May processions, the Blessed Virgin Mary is crowned by young women dressed in bridal garb. However, in this photograph from 1965, Utah State Prison inmates place a garland of flowers on the statue of Mary before regular Sunday Mass. The Catholic chaplains of the prison adapted the ritual so that young men could be a part of the quintessential May ceremony. The incarcerated, who fell outside of the Catholic parish structure, also received the care and sacramental presence of Utah's clergy. (DSLC.)

This 1969 photograph of the Catholic Charities office exemplifies an important shift in the care for the poor and marginal. The professionalization of social work during the early 20th century encouraged more local and bureaucratic organization within dioceses. In 1945, Bishop Duane Hunt incorporated Catholic Charities, and diocesan priests began to coordinate welfare activities once solely under the control of religious orders of sisters. Catholic Charities also facilitated adoptions. (DSLC.)

While priests were the executive directors of Catholic Charities that oversaw diocesan efforts, day-to-day social welfare activities remained under the auspices of women religious. In 1967, this photograph was taken of the opening of a thrift store run by the Daughters of Charity of St. Vincent de Paul. They are wearing a habit modified in 1964. (DSLC.)

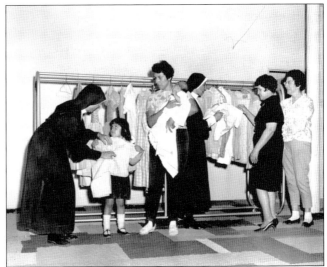

In 1959, Catholic Woman's League (CWL) members enjoy each other's company at a fundraising luncheon. Founded in 1916, the CWL provided charitable, social, and civic service in the diocese. The financial support of Catholic women not only enabled the establishment of schools and hospitals, but through organizations like the CWL, the poor, elderly, and disabled also received needed care. (USHS.)

On December 16, 1957, Frank Somogyvary and daughter Ildy were photographed arriving in Salt Lake City. They were refugees fleeing from the violence of the Hungarian Revolution. The Catholic Woman's League sponsored five families, providing them with the resources they needed to establish themselves in a new country. The women located housing, furniture, appliances, clothing, food, night schooling, and jobs for 21 people. (DSLC.)

By 1976, refugee resettlement had been taken over by Catholic Charities (later known as Catholic Community Services). The end of the Vietnam War provoked a flood of refugees, and the Catholic dioceses across the country helped resettle traumatized families. The Gao Yang family arrived in Salt Lake City from Laos. Eventually, the organization partnered with the federal government to provide immigration and refugee services. Refugee resettlement became a major focus of the diocese, and since the Vietnam War, over 60,000 refugees have come to Utah. (DSLC.)

Leaders of Utah came together in September 1932 to unveil a monument honoring the Sisters of the Holy Cross who were Catholic leaders themselves in education, health, and social welfare. Standing on the left is George H. Dern, governor of Utah, and to his right is George Albert Smith, member of the Quorum of the Twelve Apostles (the Church of Jesus Christ of Latter-day Saints) as well as president of the Utah Pioneer Trails and Landmark Association. George A. Smith would become LDS Church president in 1945. Msgr. Duane Garrison Hunt (to Smith's right) was bishop-administrator of the Diocese of Salt Lake City until James E. Kearney was consecrated in October. Hunt would become bishop in 1937. (UU.)

Five

LEADING

This carte de visite photograph may have been taken shortly after the ordination of Lawrence Scanlan (1843–1915) as bishop in 1887. Born in Ballytarsna, Ireland, Scanlan had been a priest in frontier Utah since 1873. Hardy and imposing, the bishop directed the spiritual life of the growing Catholic community. Scanlan also oversaw the foundation of churches, schools, hospitals, an orphanage, and the cathedral during his 44 years in Utah. (HC.)

8 Montgomery Street,
Opposite the Palace and Grand Hotels
San Francisco.

Denis Kiely was the constant companion of Lawrence Scanlan. Born in 1849 in Waterford, Ireland, he came to California and then was sent along with Scanlan to Utah. The two men worked closely together from 1874 to Scanlan's death in 1915. Kiely served as a pastor in several mining communities. Eventually, Kiely became cathedral rector and directed the affairs of the diocese when Scanlan was traveling. As editor of the Catholic newspaper and author of a diocesan history, he shaped the story of Utah's Catholics. Denis Kiely remained at the side of Bishop Scanlan in his last days and left the diocese shortly after the bishop's death. Father Kiely died in the home of his brother in California in 1920. (USHS.)

Utah's second bishop, Joseph S. Glass (1874–1926), was educated and refined. Glass entered the Vincentians and was ordained in 1897. After studies in Rome, he graduated with a doctor of divinity degree. Glass served as professor and president at St. Vincent's College in Los Angeles where he enjoyed the company of the affluent. In the photograph above, he stands in the "cloister" of the Los Angeles mansion of oil magnate Edward Doheny. Appointed bishop in 1915, Glass renovated the cathedral, collected art and ornate vestments, and furnished an elegant Federal Heights home. While the cathedral gained a beautifully decorated interior, it also assumed a new debt. Falling ill while visiting Los Angeles, Glass died in 1926 at the age of 51. A large funeral (below) at the cathedral occurred after his body was returned to Salt Lake City for burial. (Both, USHS.)

Within the parish, priests led their congregations with both love and a firm hand. Msgr. Alfredo F. Giovannoni (1881–1961, left) was born in Lucca, Italy. After his ordination, Giovannoni accompanied his sister's children to the United States, and eventually, he settled in Utah. Father Giovannoni served Italian- and English-speaking Catholics near Price, traveling constantly to minister to his far-flung flock. In 1930, Fr. James Early Collins (below, the priest at left center) was appointed to lead the Mexican American community at Our Lady of Guadalupe Mission. The parish priests are flanked by Sisters of Perpetual Adoration who came from Mexico in 1927. (Both, USHS.)

Without wives and children, priests made deep friendships with their fellow clergy. The dapper men above gather for a portrait at the 1928 funeral of Msgr. Michael Cushnahan. In a geographically large state with a very small Catholic population, priests were often isolated in their parishes. In the 1964 photograph below, James Fogarty, pastor of St. James Catholic Church in Vernal, greets visitors in his new rectory. (Above, DSLC; below, UCL.)

Bishop Duane Garrison Hunt (1884–1960) stands surrounded by influential Catholic men at what probably was an Easter Mass during the 1940s. The fifth bishop of the Diocese of Salt Lake, Hunt was a convert. He entered the priesthood after teaching at the University of Utah and was ordained in 1920. After eight months serving in Vernal, Hunt spent his life at the cathedral. In addition to administrative duties, he directed the cathedral choir and edited the diocesan newspaper. Beginning in 1927 and continuing even after he became bishop in 1937, Hunt presented a weekly radio program called the *Utah Catholic Hour*. He presided over Catholic postwar growth in Utah. During his time as bishop, the number of clergy rose from 35 priests in 1939 to 81 in 1957. Fifteen new parishes were founded before his death in 1960. (DSLC.)

Above, Bishop Duane Hunt stands in front of a bookmobile supported in 1942 by Catholics and the USO. The trailer contained free magazines, pamphlets, and writing materials (below). During World War II, Utah housed 14 important military installations. Hill Field, for instance, employed 15,000 civilians and 6,000 military men and women. Catholics were among the many religious groups who sought to support the troops during the war. They did not hesitate to include their own religious reading material in the bookmobile. (Both, USHS.)

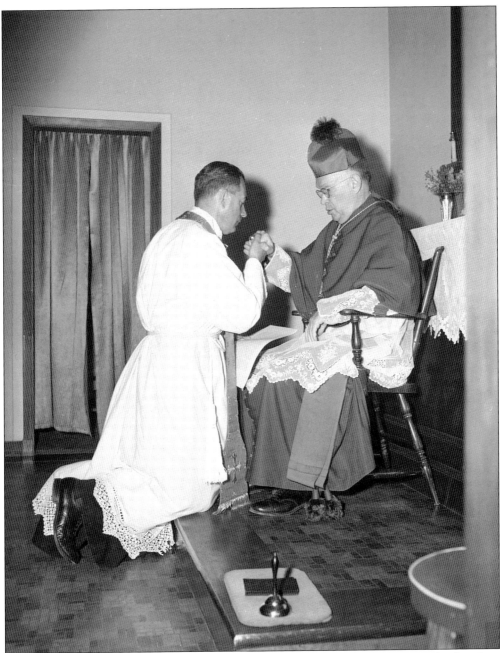

In 1951, Bishop Duane Hunt installed Fr. Ignatius Strancar as pastor of St. Helen's Church in Roosevelt. During and after World War II, more "outsiders" migrated to Utah to work in the war industry and later in the burgeoning energy sector. The Uinta Basin, where Roosevelt was located, became a focal point of petroleum operations. As Catholic congregations grew, Bishop Hunt was kept busy traveling across the state to dedicate new buildings and bless new clergy. (UCL.)

To encourage vocations to the priesthood and sisterhood, a group of laymen and laywomen formed the Serra Club. Msgr. Joseph P. Morton (left), Serra Club chaplain, and Harold O. Molitor (right), Serra Vocations Bureau member, stand in front of a portable exhibition that had vocational materials, brochures, and pamphlets. Serra Club took the display to schools, parishes, and Catholic Youth Organizations (CYO) classes. (DSLC.)

These Daughters of Charity in 1962 have brought a doll dressed in their habit to a vocations tea given by the National Council of Catholic Women. The early 1960s saw the peak number of women entering religious orders, partially because of the marketing efforts by enthusiastic sisters. (DSLC.)

Vocation teas with exhibits, like this one in 1962, sought to cultivate Catholic leadership. Girls who saw sisters as teachers might be intrigued by their dedication to Christian service. At this booth, a Franciscan Sister of the Atonement (the order that served at St. Helen's in Roosevelt) invites the curious to learn about the history and mission of the order. As with the Daughters of Charity, dolls illustrate the distinctive habits of the professed and novice sisters. (DSLC.)

Leadership among the laity was developed at three-day Cursillo retreats. After their 1964 retreat, the men of St. Rose of Lima Parish posed for a group photograph. By the mid-1960s, the number of Spanish-speaking Catholics in Utah had risen steeply, and church leaders wanted to ensure their religious commitment. The retreats also encouraged useful social activities. In 1966, the Mexican American community leased and remodeled a 7,200-foot warehouse that became the Guadalupe Center (below). At various times, it supported a credit union, a clinic, a library (reading room), an adult education program, and a restaurant. (Both, DSLC.)

In 1960, Joseph L. Federal became bishop of the Diocese of Salt Lake. Originally from North Carolina, he came to Utah in 1951 to be an auxiliary bishop. As non-Mormon growth in the state continued, Bishop Federal kept coordinating land purchases and overseeing new construction. Here, he poses with a Daughter of Charity at the 1963 groundbreaking ceremony for St. Ambrose Parish school in Salt Lake City. (DSLC.)

The 1964 dedication of a new rectory for St. James Parish in Vernal not only brought Bishop Joseph L. Federal to eastern Utah, the celebration also served as the occasion for a gathering of the region's clergy. From left to right are (first row) altar boy John Lube, Vernal; priests John Sullivan, Copperton and Laurence Spellen, Magna; two Vernal altar boys, James Pitchford and David Schwabe; and John Hedderman, a priest from Salt Lake City; (second row) priests Cornelius Monacelli and Patrick Kennedy, both from Ogden; James Godley, Evanston, Wyoming; and Francis Pellegrino, Salt Lake City; Bishop Federal; James Fogarty, pastor of St. James, Vernal; and priests Patrick McInally, Salt Lake City; Manuel Lucero, Roosevelt; and Rudolph Daz, Eureka. (UCL.)

The Catholic Church has a sacred calendar that lists many days that celebrate holy people and events. Historically, the community would come together to eat, drink, and dance. In this undated photograph, the Legion of Mary has organized children to observe St. Patrick's Day. A Catholic lay organization, the Legion of Mary was founded in 1921 in Ireland. The children are posed as if they have just finished an Irish jig. Nestled between the smiling performers is a statue of Our Lady of Fatima. (DSLC.)

Six

HAVING FUN

Catholic life in Utah included events that sought to bring together the community for entertainment and enjoyment. Having fun solidified Catholic identity by stressing the pleasurable aspects of religious commitment. In this 1904 photograph, children are enjoying their time at the Saltair playground on "Catholic Day." Saltair, a resort on the south shore of Great Salt Lake, was built in 1893 by the Mormon Church. A railroad ran from the city to this "Coney Island of the West." In addition to swimming, people could enjoy the roller coaster, merry-go-round, and Ferris wheel. The church sold the resort to Mormon businessmen in 1906. Saltair was extremely popular, but it burned to the ground in 1925. (USHS.)

For Catholics, marriage is one of seven sacraments. In addition to its religious importance, weddings also were important community events. Families were being joined to form even more families. This undated photograph, probably from the early 1920s, is of a Slovenian double wedding. Two of the Tomsic brothers married two sisters, Manda and Rosa Brjakovich. On the very top row are Mr. and Mrs. John Skerl. The wedding mass was celebrated by Fr. Alfredo F. Giovannoni, pastor of St. Anthony of Padua Church in Helper. He stands prominently above the brides. While the wedding portrait is one of staid respectability, certainly the party after the wedding mass would bring joy and excitement to all involved. For recent immigrants, weddings were pleasurable times to remember traditional foods and customs. (UU.)

For women who chose a life in the sisterhood, the delights of family and married life were exchanged for devotion to Christ and the church. Although Catholics at the time would see such devotion as the highest path toward God, the sacrifices demanded were many. Sisters, were not, however, excluded from all forms of fun. In 1917, a student at St. Mary's Academy photographed five of her teachers after they completed a game of tennis. From left to right, Sisters Bennidetta, Nunseo, Corola, Wilma, and Josepha pause at the net, holding one of their rackets. (DSLC.)

These are rare, undated snapshots of the Sisters of the Holy Cross swimming at Black Rock Resort. From the time of the Mormon pioneers of 1847, the beach on the south end of the Great Salt Lake was popular for recreational bathing. Nearby was an unusually large black rock that stood out from the shore like a tower over the flat landscape. Because the level of water in the Great Salt Lake varied, lodging could not be built, but a dock made it possible to appreciate the water. Despite their bonnets, head coverings, long sleeves, and leggings, the sisters appear to be enjoying their outing. (Both, DSLC.)

For many Catholics, precisely what sisters did when they were not teaching or nursing was a mystery. What constituted "fun" for women under vows of poverty, chastity, and obedience? In 1966, parents of parochial school children decided that as a part of Teachers' Recognition and Appreciation Day, they would treat 40 area sisters to lunch. Afterward, the parents arranged for a tour of Kennecott Copper Corporation's Magna Concentrator. The concentrator processed copper ore from Bingham Canyon Mine prior to smelting and refining. A photographer from *Intermountain Catholic* captured the sisters walking across a bridge over train tracks. (DSLC.)

Parish sports teams encouraged solidarity, physical fitness, and enjoyment. In 1966, Frank Baden (left) and Chet Pilarczyk (right) of St. Joseph's Church in Ogden offer their winning trophy to their pastor, Msgr. Patrick Kennedy. (DSLC.)

For women, parish sports teams also offered a respite from home duties and church responsibilities. These women from St. Ambrose Church called their team "St. Mary's." They won the Catholic Ladies' Bowling League championship in May 1963. From left to right, the players are Madeline Binicisz, Margaret Reagan, Madalene Crus, Helen Kelley, and Mary Crowley. (DSLC.)

During the spring of 1965, the Catholic Woman's League's organized a fashion show for one of their meetings. As with many women's clubs of the early 20th century, the Catholic Woman's League combined fundraising for charitable causes with social events, like lunches or fashion shows. The spring fashion show was organized by Vesta Seidel, a sewing instructor at St. Mary of the Wasatch College. Two of her students (Tetranella Bell, left, and Susan Granieri, right) modeled suits that they made, while others modeled sports outfits. Students Martha Fritz and Trudy Gorley (not pictured) provided commentary on the fashions while Karen Kuemmerle (not pictured) played the piano. (DSLC.)

Shortly after the Christmas holidays in 1967, Catholic women from Ogden planned an "Infant Jesus Tea." The women presented handmade layettes, a baby's first set of clothes and blankets, to Victory Noll Sisters who would give them to families in need. Catholic as well as non-Catholic women would purchase tickets for the tea and bring more baby gifts, all of which would be distributed by the Victory Noll Sisters. The tea would be held at the sisters' convent. Such events not only provided time for entertaining conversation, they also legitimized women's pastimes by connecting them with a good cause. In addition, when laywomen worked with women religious, the distance between the two groups diminished. Each group gained from supporting the other. The women are, from left to right, Mrs. B.J. Wardle of St. James Parish, Sister Mary Joan, Mrs. Vincent Bokoski of St. Mary's, and Mrs. Lewis Joseph of St. Joseph's. (DSLC.)

Women expressed their creative talent and artistic skills at fundraising bazaars. In this 1962 photograph, women proudly pose in front of crocheted blankets, carved cradles, and dolls wearing homemade clothes. At an afternoon tea, while munching on cookies, the public purchased the donated handicrafts for family or gifts. The process enabled women to give of their time, talent, and treasure—needed for a functioning Catholic community—while socializing with friends. (DSLC.)

The fundraising bazaar subsidized cloistered Carmelites who had come to Utah in 1952. Five nuns established a monastery first in Salt Lake and then in Holladay. Typically isolated from others, they lived lives of constant prayer. Consequently, it was unusual that Sister Mary Joseph would permit the *Intermountain Catholic* to photograph her with "Buck-a-Roo" bear and his rocking horse "Raspberry" to promote their 1962 fundraising bazaar. (DSLC.)

For young Catholics, having fun often included the chance to meet those of the opposite sex. Conversation, flirting, and dancing took place under the watchful eyes of school authorities. At the 1937 dance at St. Mary's of the Wasatch (above), elegant young women are accompanied by young men sporting dark suits and tuxedoes. The formality of the occasion reflects a society where youthful behavior was closely regulated. After World War II, styles and attitudes changed (below). At this dance sponsored by the Catholic Youth Organization (CYO), teens who were not going to parochial schools had a chance to meet each other. While their dress reflects the more casual world of the 1950s, it still was expected that Catholics only would marry other Catholics. Meeting Catholics in predominately Mormon Utah was not always easy, but dances helped. (Both, DSLC.)

Utah is internationally known for its skiing, which began as a popular winter sport during the 1950s. Federal funding in the early 1960s enabled Park City to establish a new ski area. At some point, St. Mary's of the Wasatch Academy came to own a cabin in the mountains where students could come and ski. Undated photographs show a substantial house and young women mastering the winter equipment. For a group of elite women, skiing became one more exciting skill they learned at school. (Both, DSLC.)

In 1966, children from parishes on the west side of the Salt Lake Valley (Immaculate Conception, St. Paschal, and St. Joseph the Worker) celebrated the December 6 feast day of Our Lady of Guadalupe. The parishes included a substantial Mexican American community. The children were dressed in Mexican-style costumes and performed the story of the Virgin Mary appearing to the peasant Juan Diego in 1531. Adults often design activities that they think children will enjoy. But are the children having fun or just the parents? (DSLC.)

On the eastern side of the state in 1955, a Christmas pageant took place at St. Helen's Church in Roosevelt. Most likely, a Ute girl is playing the role of the angel who announces to Mary that she will be the mother of the Savior. (UCL.)

Space could be made holy not only with religious rituals. Rituals of solidarity, like sharing meals, also were a part of Catholic life. In June 1954, parishioners of St. Helen's Church in Roosevelt assembled to eat together. Their parish meal served to strengthen religious identity as well as provide amusement, even if the space was tight and the parishioners few. (UCL.)

Well-established parishes like St. Joseph's in Ogden could use school facilities to put on large celebrations. In 1967, a formal dinner celebrated the Golden Jubilee of the ordination of the parish's pastor, Msgr. Patrick F. Kennedy. Tablecloths were spread across long tables complete with floral centerpieces and candles. Women wore their fancy hats, and even local Catholic sisters attended. The photograph also indicates that there were African American members of the parish (center right). (DSLC.)

In midcentury America, it was not uncommon for many religious and civic organizations to put on amateur entertainment events. Part of the fun was seeing friends and family acting on stage. In 1964, Ogden Catholics sold tickets to the "Hi-Fever Follies of '64" to raise money for St. Benedict's Hospital. To publicize the event, the organizers and stars were featured in the *Intermountain Catholic*. According to the photograph's caption, Dr. Drew M. Petersen "passes judgment on Jennifer Hull's feather bonnet." (DSLC.)

BIBLIOGRAPHY

Butler, Anne M. "Western Spaces, Catholic Places." *U.S. Catholic Historian* 18 (2000): 25–39.

Callahan, Kathryn. "Sisters of the Holy Cross and Kearns-St. Ann's Orphanage." *Utah Historical Quarterly* 78 (2010): 254–274.

Dwyer, Robert J. "Catholic Education in Utah: 1875–1975." *Utah Historical Quarterly* 43 (1975): 362–378.

———. "Pioneer Bishop: Lawrence Scanlan, 1843–1915." *Utah Historical Quarterly* 20 (1952): 135–158.

Grow, Matthew J. "The Whore of Babylon and the Abomination of Abominations: Nineteenth-Century Catholic and Mormon Mutual Perceptions and Religious Identity." *Church History* 73 (2004): 139–167.

McGloin, John Bernard. "Two Early Reports Concerning Roman Catholicism in Utah,1876–1881." *Utah Historical Quarterly* 29 (1961): 332–344.

McKay, Kathryn L. "Sisters of Ogden's Mount St. Benedict Monastery." *Utah Historical Quarterly* 77 (2009): 242–259.

Merrill, Jerald H. "Fifty Years with a Future: Salt Lake's Guadalupe Mission and Parish." *Utah Historical Quarterly* 40 (1972): 243-264.

Mooney, Bernice. "The Americanization of an Immigrant, the Rev. Msgr. Alfredo E. Giovannoni." *Utah Historical Quarterly* 60 (1992): 168–186.

Mooney, Bernice Maher. *Salt of the Earth: The History of the Catholic Church in Utah, 1776–2007.* Third edition. Salt Lake City: University of Utah Press, 2008.

Penrod, Emma Louise. "Tooele, Touch Typing, and the Catholic Saint Marguerite-Marie Alacoque." *Utah Historical Quarterly* 83 (2015): 52–59.

Topping, Gary. "Mormon-Catholic Relations in Utah History: A Sketch." *Dialogue* 51 (2018): 61–84.

Vélez de Escalante, Silvestre, and Ted J. Warner. *The Domínguez-Escalante Journal: Their Expedition Through Colorado, Utah, Arizona, and New Mexico in 1776.* Salt Lake City: University of Utah Press, 1995.

Ventilla, Andrea. "The History of Saint Mary's Academy in Salt Lake City 1875-1926." *Utah Historical Quarterly* 80 (2012): 226–241.

Discover Thousands of Local History Books Featuring Millions of Vintage Images

Arcadia Publishing, the leading local history publisher in the United States, is committed to making history accessible and meaningful through publishing books that celebrate and preserve the heritage of America's people and places.

Find more books like this at
www.arcadiapublishing.com

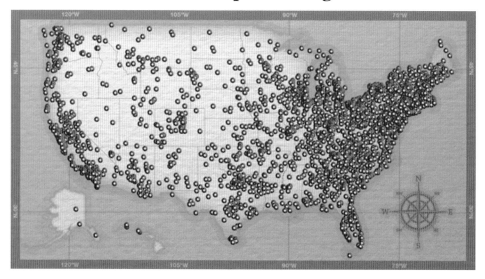

Search for your hometown history, your old stomping grounds, and even your favorite sports team.